Over 50 Mediterranean Marijuana Meals

Baked
Italian

By Yzabetta Sativa

GREEN CANDY PRESS

BAKED ITALIAN: Over 50 Mediterranean Marijuana Meals

Published by Green Candy Press

San Francisco, CA

Copyright © 2013 Yzabetta Sativa

ISBN 978-1-937866-18-1

Photographs © Brody Bruce

Printed in China by Oceanic Graphic International Inc.

Sometimes Massively Distributed by P.G.W.

Contents

Introduction

Growing up in the Italian section of Montréal, I developed an affinity for Italian food at a young age. Pasta always made a great main dish for my brothers with their insatiable appetites, and the agreeable starch made for a healthy athletic diet. For me it was always the sauces that could magically turn an insipid dish of dough into a magnificent meal.

I grew up with two biological brothers and five foster brothers and they all played hockey. Athletes benefit the most from the amount of carbohydrates they have stored in their body, and the fact that pasta is so easy to cook in large amounts meant that it was perfect for our family. For this reason we had some form of pasta at least three times a week. All the boys loved Italian food and it was the first food my mom learned to cook, so the other four days a week we often had other Italian dishes, too.

We all grew up together in the '70s and early '80s. We all smoked pot with one apparatus or another, and I know for a fact that when it came to stoner food my brothers always preferred Italian, hands down. It was a very communal event when we'd all crowd in the kitchen at night after smoking ourselves silly, some of us working on the sauce, some making the other courses and some on guard, keeping us all quiet so we didn't wake up our parents. Other times, the parents were out coaching hockey teams that none of my brothers played on so it was relatively easy to get away with these meals.

In the kitchen we'd laugh a lot, as one is prone to doing after getting high. We'd cook, we'd eat together and then we'd all hang out in the basement while one played a beat up old acoustic and a few others would screech out Rush tunes. These half-assed jam sessions make up some of my fondest memories of my wasted adolescence.

Recently, I gathered all my brothers together over a big Italian meal (what else?) and we reminisced about these times. We all agreed that while it was textbook dysfunction in many regards, we all remember those fabulous Italian meals with high regard. For me, they are much fonder memories than the ones I have of spending ten months of the year in a cold, rusty ice rink drinking the most god-awful cups of what should not be called hot chocolate out of vending machines.

This collection of all my brothers' favorite recipes is a celebration of my misspent youth and all the wonderful dishes we shared together. Many of the recipes are classics straight out of my mom's grease-stained recipe box. Some of these recipes she cooked over and over, some of them come from the brothers' kitchens, and some of them have my own personal flourishes on them. *Buon appetito!*

A Wee Bit About Weed

I do most, if not all of my baking, with what is affectionately called BC Bud. Thing is, it is actually grown locally and hydroponically and doesn't come from British Columbia. BC Bud has been parented by a British Columbian clone that sometimes is referred to as White Widow because of how caked the flowers are. This particular strain of weed is a 60% indica, 40% sativa hybrid that is lusciously heady and altogether charming.

Here in Canada there's a lot of smack talk about pot (seeing as how it's our second largest agricultural crop), so it's hard to believe anything about the infamous "White Widow." My botanically dense, plant-killer mentality thinks that it's really one sub strain or another of Northern Lights – but don't quote me on that.

Indica buds are compact, weighty, short and fat. The thing with indicas is that they smell "skunky" and their smoke is so thick that a small toke can induce coughing. The best indicas have a tranquil sort of "social high" which makes one chill and take in the scenery rather than pseudo-philosophically analyze the scenery to dullard death.

Sativa, on the other hand, has long, medium-thick buds that smell more tangy than sweet; if indica smells "skunky," then sativa smells like dirt or mud. The smoke is smooth and gives a kind of frenetic and confusing high. In short; sativa gets you high and indica gets you stoned. That's pretty much the extent of my scientific knowledge of weed botany.

The most anyone really know goes as follows: most of the THC, the medicinal ingredient, is in the flower buds of the female cannabis plant, with some in the leaves too. When I make Baked Butter I use the flower buds of really good pot. One could use the leaves or the stalk as well as what is known as "shake," but you wouldn't get as potent a butter as may be your intended goal. It's a personal choice.

The Disclaimer

Marijuana is illegal whether you smoke it or cook with it if you don't have a prescription for it

Do not eat cannabis and drive. Do not drink and drive. Hell, don't bother driving at all if you can help it, because it puts unnecessary wrinkles on your face.

Know your tolerance, whether you have never tried pot or have been using copious amounts for years. The first time you try eating cannabis-laced food you should eat just a small amount and wait for an hour and a half. At that point you will be feeling the effects of the THC; take note of how you feel and the next time you ingest, adjust the dosage. Always eat the amount recommended in each of the recipes, not more. Eating marijuana gives the same effects as smoking it, but often lasts two or three times longer, which you should keep in mind at all times.

Don't eat pot on an empty stomach. Sure, some people will tell you it's better on an empty stomach but in my opinion it's best to have something to eat beforehand. Even a glass of milk is a good start. Having something in your stomach seems to help prevent you from eating too much or getting hit too hard. To quote Martha Stewart, "It's a good thing."

You must be patient; don't just keep eating your medicated pasta until you feel the effects. I can't say this enough: it will take a while for it to hit you. Make very sure that when you get the munchies you don't eat more. Please do not create a six- or eight-course Italian feast and have every dish include some form of pot. The dishes in this book are designed for consumption with other dishes that don't contain cannabis. If you're making an eight-course extravaganza based on the courses outlined in this book, just have one course include a cannabis-laden dish. Care must be exercised, as the delayed response time when eating pot can encourage overdosing in people who are not used to ingesting marijuana. If you eat too much pot you can feel very rough; experiencing panic and anxiety reactions is bad enough, but you can also have to endure physical discomfort, too.

Absorption of THC though the stomach is slower than through the lungs, which is why you need to be patient.

It can take well over an hour and a half to be absorbed into the body and for you to feel "high." THC gets absorbed at a different rate every time you eat it. The effects of eating cannabis can last several hours, while they tend to wear off within an hour when smoked. If you fall asleep or pass out please remember that your digestion will slow down, which means you could wake up still high.

Make no mistake, you can eat far too much pot and the results of that are unpleasant, to say the least. If you do have a dose that is really too high, it can last a long time, possibly as long as ten hours. This is not as fun as it sounds; if you're in the wrong place or with the wrong people it can become very upsetting and you can even pass out. Pot is meant to be fun and relaxing, and dizziness, sweating, nausea, vomiting, possible crying and freaking out are definitely not fun.

If you do eat too much there are a couple of things you can do. Stay low to the ground, to avoid nasty head rushes, and try taking a high dose of vitamin C (200mg or more) to help to make you feel better. You can also try eating something relatively heavy—a slice of pizza rather than a salad—or something quite sugary. The best antidote is to crawl into bed and go to sleep.

You, as the consumer, have responsibility in three areas: your situation, health and safety. The situational responsibilities include the avoidance of risky situations, not using it when you're alone and not using it because someone persuasive talked you into it. Health responsibilities include not eating too much or mixing it with other drugs, attentiveness to all the possible health consequences of drug use and not using a drug recreationally during periods of excessive stress in order to self medicate. If you are self-medicating, in my opinion you have a problem that eating pot isn't going to help. Safety-related responsibilities include using the smallest dose necessary to achieve the desired effects, using only in laid back surroundings with supportive friends and not doing anything ridiculous like operating heavy machinery after eating pot.

I am highlighting responsible drug use as a chief prevention technique in my personal harm-reduction drug policy and because I care. We all want to enjoy pot, so just don't be stupid and have fun!

Extractions

Baked Butter

It doesn't get better than this

Place the powdered pot and butter or margarine in a regular crock pot. A mini crock pot (1½-quart) is the best. Regular size crock pots are only good if you're cooking 3 or 4 pounds of Baked Butter or margarine at a time.

Heat the butter or margarine and powdered pot together in the crock pot on low for at least 12 hours but ultimately for 24 hours, covered. Allow the butter or margarine to cool then strain through a strainer, lined with a layer of cheesecloth, into a large bowl. Twist the pulp left in the double layer of cheesecloth to get out all the liquid butter or margarine that you can. Refrigerate to quicken cooling. When cool, cut into large pieces, then place Baked Butter or margarine in sandwich bags for freezing in ½ cup quantities.

I personally don't strain the butter or margarine when it's done, if not out of abject laziness then for the added fiber in my diet. The only thing you have to be careful of, if you choose not to strain, is that a ½ cup of butter or margarine with the powdered pot in it does not actually measure a ½ cup of butter or margarine. I measure ½ a cup plus a dollop, if you will, to even out the score.

It used to be that people would use "shake" or low-grade pot for making Baked Butter. However, more recent studies show that the superiority,

INGREDIENTS

1 pound of butter or margarine (margarine just doesn't work the same but if you're vegan or lactose intolerant then by all means, use vegan margarine)

½ ounce of good pot ground to a powder (You can grind the pot up by using a coffee grinder, pepper grinder or blender, though when I do it in a blender I add the butter or margarine, melted, to the blender.)

To begin, you will need the pot and the butter.

Grind the pot to a fine powder using a coffee grinder.

Place ingredients into a small crock pot on low heat.

Allow ingredients to melt together, then simmer for over 24 hours.

Over a bowl, pour the ingredients into a strainer.

Squeeze the liquid through, and let the Baked Butter cool.

potency and staying power of the final product are greatly improved by using good pot as opposed to "shake." In Canada we're able to purchase some wonderful, hydroponically grown pot, which is my personal preference.

This Baked Butter or margarine will keep a long time in the freezer and you can use it just as you would use any butter or margarine in any recipe, be it a savory or sweet recipe. You can enjoy it in smaller amounts spread on your toast, on your pancakes or drizzled over popcorn. Each person only needs about 2 teaspoons of Baked Butter or margarine to get totally baked.

'Oregano' Oil
An infusion with a real kick!

Place the powdered pot and oil in a regular crock pot. A mini crock pot (1½-quart) is the best. Regular size crock pots are only good if you're making a lot of 'Oregano' Oil at a time. Make sure the heat on the crock pot is set at the lowest it can go.

Heat the oil and powdered pot together in the crock pot on low for at least 12 hours but ultimately for 24 hours, covered. Allow the oil to cool then strain through a strainer, lined with a layer of cheesecloth, into a large bowl. Twist pulp in the double layer of cheesecloth to get out all the oil that you can. Refrigerate to quicken cooling. When cool cut into large pieces, and place 'Oregano' Oil in sandwich bags for freezing in ⅓ cup quantities.

I personally don't strain the oil when it's done if not out of abject laziness then for the added fiber in my diet. The only thing you have to be careful of, if you choose not to strain, is that ⅓ of a cup of 'Oregano' Oil with the powdered pot in it does not actually measure ⅓ of a cup of 'Oregano' Oil. I measure ⅓ a cup plus a bit more, if you will, to even out the score.

It used to be that people would use "shake" or low grade pot for making cannabutters and oils. However, more recent studies show that the superiority, potency and staying power of the final product are greatly improved

INGREDIENTS
2 cups of olive oil

½ ounce of good pot ground to a powder (grind the pot up by using a coffee grinder)

by using good pot as opposed to "shake." In Canada we're able to purchase some wonderful, hydroponically grown pot, which is my personal preference.

This 'Oregano' Oil will keep a long time in the freezer and you can use it just as you would use any butter or margarine in any recipe, be it a savory or sweet recipe. You can enjoy it in the same regard that you would any other oil. Olive oil is the main cooking oil in countries surrounding the Mediterranean Sea.

Extra virgin olive oil is mostly used as a salad dressing and as an ingredient in salad dressings. It is also used with foods to be eaten cold. If uncompromised by heat, the flavor is stronger. It also can be used for sautéing. Some baking calls for oil instead of butter or margarine, in which case you could use 'Oregano' Oil.

N.B. You can substitute canola, peanut, sunflower, corn, vegetable or coconut oil for the olive oil.

Marijuana Milk

Bringing a whole new meaning to the concept of milk and cookies

Place the powdered pot and milk in a regular crock pot. Set the crock pot on high until the milk is just about to boil, then turn the temperature down to low.

Crock pots take an hour or two to get to the boiling stage, so you can always speed up the process by heating up the milk in the microwave or in a pot on the stove before adding it to the crock pot with the weed.

Heat the milk and powdered pot together in the crock pot on low for at least 10 hours, stirring every hour.

When the milk is infused, it will become a medium brownish color, not unlike coffee mocha or the color of a Brown Cow. If the milk is still a beige color, keep it cooking for longer.

Allow the milk to cool then strain through a strainer lined with a layer of cheesecloth into a large bowl. Twist the pulp in the double layer of cheesecloth to get out all the liquid. Refrigerate once the milk has cooled. Store in the refrigerator.

INGREDIENTS

½ ounce of good pot ground to a powder (grind the pot up by using a coffee grinder)

10 cups of milk (use whole milk or half-and-half, as it's the fat that brings out the THC)

Cannabis Campari

An Italian classic...with a twist

The pot you're using must be dry. When fresh pot is used, the end result has a tendency to be substandard.

If possible use an empty 1.5 liter wine bottle with a screw top lid.

Pour the Campari and ground pot into the empty wine bottle or another container. Keep the empty Campari bottle for later. Screw the lid tightly onto the bottle and let it sit for four weeks at room temperature in a dark cabinet. Twice a week you need to shake the bottle up so as to agitate the pot.

Using a coffee filter or fine sieve, strain the pot from the liqueur. Put the liqueur back into its original bottle and screw the lid on tightly.

It's best to keep the Cannabis Campari in a cool dark place to protect it from degradation by light.

As this extract is alcoholic, you need to be careful with your consumption; because it's alcohol with cannabis in it, you need to be even more careful. For every alcoholic beverage you drink make sure you drink a pint of water – and this goes for alcohol without weed in it, too!

INGREDIENTS

1 bottle of Campari (750ml)

½ ounce of good pot (ground to a powder)

Vector Vodka

A knockout in
every single shot

The pot you're using must be dry. When fresh pot is used, the end result has a tendency to be substandard.

If possible, use an empty 1.5 liter wine bottle with a screw top lid.

Pour the vodka and ground pot into the empty wine bottle. Keep the empty vodka bottle for later. Screw the lid tightly onto the bottle and let it sit for two weeks at room temperature in a dark cabinet. Twice a week you need to shake the bottle up so as to agitate the pot.

Using a coffee filter or fine sieve, strain the pot from the vodka. Put the vodka back into its original bottle and screw the lid tightly onto the bottle.

It's best to keep the Vector Vodka in a cool dark place to protect it from degradation by light.

As this extract is alcoholic, you need to be careful with your consumption; because it's alcohol with cannabis in it, you need to be even more careful. For every alcoholic beverage you drink make sure you drink a pint of water – and this goes for alcohol without weed in it, too!

INGREDIENTS

750ml bottle of vodka (of the highest proof possible in your area)

½ ounce of good pot (ground to a powder)

Ganja Gin

Mama's favorite drink

The pot you're using must be dry. When fresh pot is used, the end result has a tendency to be substandard.

If possible, use an empty 1.5 liter wine bottle with a screw top lid.

Pour the gin and ground pot into the empty wine bottle. Keep the empty gin bottle for later. Screw the lid tightly onto the bottle and let it sit for two weeks at room temperature in a dark cabinet. Twice a week you need to shake the bottle up so as to agitate the pot.

Using a coffee filter or fine sieve, strain the pot from the gin. Put the gin back into its original bottle and screw the lid tightly onto the bottle.

It's best to keep the Ganja Gin in a cool dark place to protect it from degradation by light.

As this extract is alcoholic, you need to be careful with your consumption; because it's alcohol with cannabis in it, you need to be even more careful. For every alcoholic beverage you drink make sure you drink a pint of water – and this goes for alcohol without weed in it, too!

INGREDIENTS

750ml bottle of gin (of the highest proof possible in your area)

½ ounce of good pot (ground to a powder)

Aperitivo

Aperitivo is the Italian version of an aperitif, which is a drink, usually alcoholic, served before a meal and meant to stimulate the appetite. These drinks are most often served with a little bite to eat such as olives and nuts.

Martini 31

Cardinale 33

Americano 35

Negroni 37

Rosemary Baked Olives 39

Peppered Nuts 41

Martini

Shaken, not stirred – although you will be!

Into a mixing glass, toss in the 6 ice cubes then pour in the Ganja Gin and the vermouth.

Stir well.

Strain and pour into a martini glass.

To finish, either drop a couple of green olives into the bottom of the martini glass, or arrange a twist of lemon peel on the edge of the martini glass.

For every alcoholic beverage you drink make sure you drink at least one pint of water. One glass of Martini should be more than enough to get you baked.

INGREDIENTS

2 ounces of Ganja Gin

¼ ounce of dry vermouth

1 to 3 green olives OR a twist of lemon peel

6 ice cubes

Cardinale

The perfect mix of
bud and bitters

Fill an old fashioned glass with ice. Pour all ingredients over the ice and serve.

For every alcoholic beverage you drink make sure you drink at least one pint of water. One glass of Cardinale should be more than enough to get you baked.

INGREDIENTS

2 ounces of Ganja Gin

½ ounce of dry vermouth

½ ounce of Cannabis Campari

ice

Americano

A sip of home with
the taste of Italy!

Fill a medium-sized tumbler or a highball glass with ice. Pour the Cannabis Campari and the vermouth into the tumbler. Top the glass off with club soda.

Garnish with a lemon twist or a slice of orange.

For every alcoholic beverage you drink make sure you drink at least one pint of water. One glass of Americano should be more than enough to get you baked.

INGREDIENTS

1 ounce of Cannabis Campari

1 ounce of sweet vermouth

club soda

a lemon twist or orange slice
    for garnish

ice

Negroni

The flavor
of Florence

Fill a highball glass three quarters of the way with ice; cracked ice works best. Pour all the ingredients over the ice. You can add a splash of club soda but it's optional.

Garnish with the blood orange slice.

For every alcoholic beverage you drink make sure you drink at least one pint of water. One glass of Negroni should be more than enough to get you baked.

INGREDIENTS

1 ounce of Ganja Gin

1 ounce of sweet vermouth

1 ounce of Cannabis Campari

ice

slice of blood orange

Rosemary Baked Olives

You'll be more baked than they are!

Preheat your oven to 375°F.

In a 12 by 12-inch baking dish, stir the olives together with the wine, lemon juice, 'Oregano' Oil and garlic. Place the sprigs of rosemary in between the olives.

Bake the olives in the preheated oven for 15 minutes, stirring them when they are halfway through the baking.

When you take the olives out of the oven discard the rosemary sprigs, then stir in the parsley, oregano, lemon orange zest, and red pepper flakes. Serve warm.

This recipe is enough to get 4 people baked.

INGREDIENTS

4 tablespoons of 'Oregano' Oil

3 cloves of garlic, finely chopped

4 sprigs of fresh rosemary

2 tablespoons of chopped, fresh parsley

2 tablespoons of chopped, fresh oregano

3 teaspoons of grated lemon zest

¼ teaspoon of crushed red pepper flakes

5 cups of whole mixed black and green olives, drained

½ cup of Pinot Grigio

2 tablespoons fresh squeezed lemon juice

Peppered Nuts

A treat that's hot in
more ways than one

Preheat your oven to 250°F.

Melt the Baked Butter in a medium frying pan, then add Tabasco sauce, garlic and salt and pepper. Sauté these ingredients together for about 2 minutes, just until they're well combined.

Toss the nuts in with the Baked Butter mixture and stir them briefly over the heat until the nuts are all well coated. Spread the nuts and butter out in a single layer on a baking sheet.

Bake the nuts for about 1 hour or until they become crispy. Make sure you stir them every 10 to 15 minutes to keep them from burning.

Serve them whenever you'd like. This recipe is enough to get 6 people baked.

INGREDIENTS

½ cup of Baked Butter

4 cloves of garlic, minced

2 teaspoons of Tabasco sauce

½ teaspoon of salt

1 teaspoon of cracked black
    pepper

2 cups of whole almonds

2 cups of hazelnuts

2 cups of pistachios

Antipasto

The *antipasto* is the slightly heavier starter course. It is usually cold (not in all cases) and lighter than the first course. It is an appetizer usually consisting of an assortment of foods.

Crostini 45

Beef Carpaccio 47

Lamb Carpaccio 49

Eggplant Parmesan 51

Antipasto Salad 53

Stuffed Peppers 55

Crostini

A delicious addition to any spread

Preheat oven to 375°F.

Slice baguettes on the diagonal into ¼-inch slices.

Brush both sides of the bread rounds with 'Oregano' Oil. Rub both sides with raw garlic cloves, scraping the garlic into the bread.

Arrange on a baking sheet. Salt and pepper the top sides of the bread slices.

Bake the Crostini for at least 10 minutes, turning over at the halfway mark, or until crisp and golden on the surface, but not hard-toasted all the way through.

These Crostini can be served hot or at room temperature. This recipe makes enough to get 4-6 people baked.

INGREDIENTS

2 baguettes or similar multigrain
   loaves
⅓ cup of 'Oregano' Oil
2 cloves of garlic
sea salt and cracked black pepper
   to taste

Beef Carpaccio

Named after an Italian painter,

this dish is a work of art

Use a vegetable peeler to make thin shavings of Parmesan and set them aside.
Pound out the thin beef tenderloin slices until they're very thin.

Lay a circle of arugula on a platter. Top each piece of arugula with one slice of the Beef Carpaccio. Top the beef with one slice of the Parmesan. Sprinkle the Carpaccio with the chopped capers. Drizzle all over with the 'Oregano' Oil and sprinkle with salt and pepper.

Allow to stand for 20 minutes. Serve with Crostini and lemon wedges on the side. This recipe is enough to get 4-6 people baked.

INGREDIENTS

⅓ cup of 'Oregano' Oil

1 pound of beef tenderloin, trimmed of fat and sinew, cut into ⅛-inch slices

2 cups of arugula leaves, washed, dried and torn into pieces

3 ounces of freshly grated Parmesan cheese

6-8 lemon wedges

2 tablespoons of chopped capers

sea salt and freshly ground pepper to taste

Lamb Carpaccio

A favorite in my house;
the taste of family dinner!

Pound out the thin lamb loin slices until they're very thin.

Lay a circle of arugula on a platter. Top each piece of arugula with one slice of the Lamb Carpaccio. Sprinkle with chopped olives. Drizzle the 'Oregano' Oil over the lamb to taste along with the sea salt and cracked black pepper.

Scatter the crumbled feta over the Carpaccio and top with mint. Place the lemon wedges on the platter and serve immediately.

Let stand for 20 minutes. Serve with Crostini and lemon wedges on the side. This recipe is enough to get 4-6 people baked.

INGREDIENTS

⅓ cup of 'Oregano' Oil

1 pound of boneless lamb loin, trimmed of fat and sinew, cut into ⅛-inch slices

2 cups of arugula leaves, washed, dried and torn into pieces

6 ounces of feta cheese, crumbled

15 fresh mint leaves

24 Kalamata olives, chopped

6-8 lemon wedges

sea salt and freshly ground pepper to taste

Eggplant Parmesan
Creamy, delicious and
guaranteed to get you high

Preheat oven to 350°F.

Lay the sliced eggplant out on a paper towel. Sprinkle the eggplant with salt and allow to stand for 30 minutes. When the time is up wipe the eggplant off with a paper towel but do not run it under water.

Fry the eggplant slices to a light brown using the 'Oregano' Oil in a large frying pan. Remove from oil and allow to cool.

In a medium bowl mix the ricotta, mozzarella and Parmesan cheeses. Mix in egg and basil.

In a 13 by 9-inch glass baking dish, evenly spread the marinara sauce. Arrange a single layer of eggplant slices on top of the sauce. Top the eggplant with ½ of the cheese mixture. Repeat layering process until all the eggplant and cheese mixture is used. Pour remaining sauce on top of layers, and sprinkle with remaining Parmesan cheese.

Bake the eggplant for 30 to 45 minutes until the sauce is bubbly. Allow to stand for 5 minutes, then serve. This recipe is enough to get 4 people baked.

INGREDIENTS

⅓ cup of 'Oregano' Oil

6 eggplants, cut into ¼-inch slices

2 cups of ricotta cheese

⅔ cup of shredded mozzarella cheese

¼ cup of grated Parmesan cheese

1 egg, beaten

⅓ cup of chopped fresh basil

6 cups of marinara sauce

sea salt

Antipasto Salad

A plethora of delicious savory bites

In a blender, combine the marinara sauce, 'Oregano' Oil, vinegar, sugar, salt, oregano, garlic and pepper and blend until the dressing is smooth. Set aside.

Place the lettuce on a large, rimmed serving platter. Arrange the salami, cheeses, tomatoes and olives over the top in an appealing manner. Presentation counts with this salad. Sprinkle the whole platter with chives.

Just before serving drizzle the blended dressing over the salad. This recipe is enough to get 4-6 people baked.

INGREDIENTS

½ cup of salami, julienned

½ cup of Provolone cheese, julienned

1 cup of shredded mozzarella cheese

3 medium tomatoes, chopped

1 can of pitted ripe olives, drained and sliced

3 tablespoons of minced chives

1 cup of marinara sauce

⅓ cup of 'Oregano' Oil

¼ cup of white wine vinegar

½ teaspoon of brown sugar

1 teaspoon of salt

1½ teaspoons of dried oregano

½ teaspoon of finely minced garlic

¼ teaspoon of pepper

6 cups of torn romaine lettuce leaves

Stuffed Peppers

They're stuffed;
you'll be loaded

Preheat the oven to 375°F.

Heat 1 tablespoon of the 'Oregano' Oil in a medium frying pan over moderate heat. Add the onion and sauté until soft and sweet, after about 5 minutes. Set aside.

In a mixing bowl combine the onion, breadcrumbs, tomato, cheese, anchovies, almonds, mint and 2 tablespoons of 'Oregano' Oil. Stir well, then season with salt and pepper.

Arrange the peppers so that they are standing up with the open end facing up in a shallow, oiled baking dish. Fill each pepper with the breadcrumb mixture equally.

Drizzle with the remaining 1 tablespoon of 'Oregano' Oil.

Bake until well browned and crisp on top, after about 30 minutes.

Serve warm or at room temperature, but not hot. This recipe is enough to get 4 people baked.

INGREDIENTS

4 tablespoons of 'Oregano' Oil
1 small onion, minced
³/₄ cup of fine breadcrumbs
½ cup of finely chopped tomato
½ cup of freshly grated Parmesan
2 tablespoons of chopped fresh mint
8 anchovy filets, chopped
sea salt and freshly ground pepper
   to taste
4 large red bell peppers, seeded

Primo

Usually there are several pasta choices in what is considered the first course, the *primo*. Primo dishes usually consist of hot food and the foods are heavier than the antipasto, but lighter than the second course. It usually consists of non-protein foods.

Spaghetti Marinara 59

Tomato and Olive Sauce 61

Capellini with Anchovies and Lemon Sauce 63

Butterflies with Peas 65

Penne with Eggplant 67

Penne with Mandorla Sauce 69

Zucchini and Tomato Gratin 71

Polenta with Tomato Sauce 73

Spaghetti Marinara

Just like Mama used to make!

Sauté the sliced onions and garlic in the olive oil over medium heat for about 3 minutes or until they're soft and the garlic has disappeared. Add the can of tomatoes, turn up the heat and cook quickly for 3 minutes. Lower the heat at that point and let the sauce simmer for about an hour.

Chop the anchovies and add them to the sauce along with cracked black pepper, a small pinch of sea salt and the sugar. Allow to simmer for another 10 minutes then add the oregano. Keep warm over a low heat until ready to serve.

Cook the spaghetti in salted water until tender. Drain, then serve in a large, heated platter (with preheated individual plates on the side). Pour marinara sauce over the still hot spaghetti and sprinkle the grated Romano cheese over the top.

Serve immediately or divide the sauce into 4 servings. This recipe is enough to get 4 people baked.

INGREDIENTS

1 pound of spaghetti

28-ounce can of plum tomatoes

⅓ cup of 'Oregano' Oil

2 sliced onions

2 cloves of minced garlic

2 filets of anchovies

¼ teaspoon of sugar

¼ cup of grated Romano cheese

1 teaspoon of dried oregano

sea salt and cracked black pepper
  to taste

Primo

Tomato and Olive Sauce

A complex and delicious take on the classic sauce

In a food processor or blender place the olives, parsley and garlic and chop roughly. Be careful to make sure you only chop the ingredients and no more. Add the remaining ingredients and process for a second or two to combine.

Cook the spaghetti in sea-salted water until tender. Drain and serve the spaghetti in a large, heated bowl (with preheated individual plates on the side). Pour the olive sauce over the still hot spaghetti. Add chopped tomatoes and toss again.

Serve immediately or divide the sauce into 4 servings. This recipe is enough to get 4 people baked.

INGREDIENTS

1 pound of spaghetti

⅓ cup of 'Oregano' Oil

2 cloves of garlic

12-ounce jar of Spanish olives, drained

juice of 2 lemons

¼ cup of fresh parsley, chopped

2 fresh Roma tomatoes, chopped

cracked black pepper to taste

Capellini with Anchovies and Lemon Sauce

A comforting dish with a fishy tang!

Melt the Baked Butter and 'Oregano' Oil together in a saucepan. Stir in the garlic and chopped anchovies and cook for about 2 minutes. Add the parsley, salt and pepper and stir. Add the lemon juice and cook for another 2 minutes.

Cook the capellini in sea-salted water until tender. Drain and serve the capellini on a large, heated platter (with preheated individual plates on the side). Pour the anchovy sauce over the still hot capellini. Generously sprinkle the grated Parmesan cheese over the top.

Serve immediately or divide the sauce into 6 servings. This recipe is enough to get 6 people baked.

INGREDIENTS

1 pound of capellini (skinny spaghetti)

⅓ cup of 'Oregano' Oil

¼ cup of Baked Butter

12 filets of anchovy, minced

3 tablespoons of fresh parsley, chopped

1 tablespoon of fresh-squeezed lemon juice

¼ cup of Parmesan cheese, grated

sea salt and cracked black pepper to taste

Butterflies with Peas

Bacon and Parmesan mean that
this dish is more than it seems

Farfalline actually means butterflies. When I was a little girl my mom called this "Butterflies with Peas" and I still use that moniker today.

In a saucepan or wok cook the onions in 'Oregano' Oil for about 5 minutes. Add the chopped bacon and cook for just long enough to heat the bacon up. Add the parsley and garlic and stir, then add the water, peas, salt and pepper and cook slowly for about 25 minutes or until the peas are cooked.

In a separate bowl, cook the farfalline in sea-salted water until tender. Drain, then add to the pea sauce and add the grated Parmesan cheese. Turn the heat off and toss thoroughly.

Serve in large heated serving bowl along with preheated individual bowls. Serve very hot to 4 people or divide the sauce into 4 servings. This recipe is enough to get 4 people baked.

INGREDIENTS

1 pound of farfalline (small bow-tie pasta)

2 strips of bacon, cooked, drained and chopped

2 sliced onions

1/3 cup of 'Oregano' Oil

3 tablespoons of fresh parsley, chopped

2 cups of freshly shelled peas (use frozen when peas are out of season)

1 clove of garlic, minced

1/2 cup of Parmesan cheese, grated

sea salt and cracked black pepper to taste

Penne with Eggplant
A lighter take on the
traditional combination

In a saucepan heat the 'Oregano' Oil; add the garlic, onion and parsley and cook for about 3 minutes. Add the tomatoes, sea salt and cracked black pepper and let simmer for almost an hour. Stir regularly.

While the sauce is simmering, cut the eggplant into slices an inch thick, then sprinkle with sea salt. Put them in a colander and allow the moisture to drain off for about 15 minutes. Wipe the slices off and pat them dry with paper towel but do not rinse under water. Eggplant is like a sponge; if you rinse it, it will absorb the water and be mushy when cooked.

Fry the slices in hot peanut oil for about 3 minutes on each side or until the side reaches a nice golden brown color. Set the cooked slices aside and keep them hot.

Cook the penne in sea-salted water until tender. Drain, then serve the penne on a large, heated platter (with preheated individual plates on the side). Pour the tomato sauce over the still hot penne. Cut the eggplant into strips, arrange the strips over the tomato sauce and generously sprinkle the grated Parmesan cheese over the top.

Serve immediately or divide the sauce into 4 servings. This recipe is enough to get 4 people baked.

INGREDIENTS

1 pound of penne

1 large eggplant

28-ounce can of tomatoes

⅓ cup of 'Oregano' Oil

2 cloves of garlic

1 minced onion

⅓ cup of fresh parsley, chopped

⅓ cup of peanut oil

½ cup of Parmesan cheese, grated

sea salt and cracked black pepper
    to taste.

Penne with Mandorla Sauce

Sweet and nutty accents make this not your usual tomato sauce

Heat the 'Oregano' Oil in a medium saucepan over medium heat. Add the garlic and cook until it is a light golden brown in color, which should take less than 2 minutes. Add the almonds to the saucepan and cook them for another 2 minutes or until they are lightly golden brown.

Cook the penne in sea-salted water until tender. Drain.

In a food processor or blender place the almonds and peppers and combine with broth, tomato paste, parsley, vinegar, salt, sugar and pepper. Blend until the mixture is pureed. Transfer to a large heated serving bowl.

Toss the hot, drained penne with the sauce. Serve hot, warm or room temperature. Serve immediately or divide the sauce into 4 servings. This recipe is enough to get 4 people baked.

INGREDIENTS

1 pound of penne

⅓ cup of 'Oregano' Oil

4 cloves of garlic, minced

½ cup of almonds, slivered

2 cups of roasted red peppers

½ cup of chicken broth

3 tablespoons of tomato paste

1 tablespoon of red wine vinegar

¼ of a cup of fresh parsley, chopped

½ teaspoon of sugar

sea salt and cracked black pepper to taste

Zucchini and Tomato Gratin

A blend of beautiful cheeses
makes this vegetable dish come to life

Preheat oven to 375°F. Move an oven rack into the top third of the oven.

Heat the 'Oregano' Oil in a large frying pan over medium heat, and spread the zucchini slices into the pan in a single layer. If they don't fit you will have to cook them in batches, or use two frying pans, otherwise the zucchini will get mushy.

Sprinkle the crushed garlic over the zucchini and cook until the zucchini are golden brown on both sides, about 8 minutes per side. Remove them from the frying pan.

Arrange the slices of zucchini in a 9 x 12-inch glass baking dish. Build up layers in the pan by alternating the zucchini with slices of mozzarella cheese and slices of tomato, so that the slices overlap each other in a neat pattern of rows. Sprinkle the Parmesan cheese and basil over the top layer of the dish, and season to taste with salt and pepper.

Bake in the preheated oven until the cheese is melted and brown and the dish is bubbling. This should take about 30 minutes. This recipe is enough to get 4 people baked.

INGREDIENTS

⅓ cup of 'Oregano' Oil

6 zucchini, sliced

2 large cloves garlic, crushed

8 ounces of mozzarella cheese, sliced thinly

6 large tomatoes, peeled and sliced

½ cup of Parmesan cheese, grated

3 tablespoon of fresh basil, chopped

sea salt and freshly ground black pepper

Polenta with Tomato Sauce

A robust but simple meal
to enjoy with friends

In a small bowl, whisk together 2 cups of the water with the cornmeal and salt. Bring the remaining 4 cups of water to a boil in a heavy saucepan, then stir the cornmeal into it, being careful. Turn the heat to very low and cook the polenta for 40 minutes, stirring with a wooden spoon every 10 minutes. When it's done, take the pot off the heat and stir in the Baked Butter.

Make the sauce while the polenta is cooking. Heat the 'Oregano' Oil in a large saucepan over medium heat and add the onions. Cook the onions for about 5 minutes, stirring often, until they have softened but not started to brown. Stir in the chopped mushrooms and the garlic and stir the mixture over a medium heat for 5 minutes. Add the marinara sauce, sherry, chili flakes and oregano. When the sauce comes to a boil turn the heat to low. Allow the sauce to simmer for 30 minutes. When the sauce is done, season it with the sea salt and pepper.

Sprinkle the green onions and grated Parmesan cheese into the polenta. Mound the polenta on plates, make a well in the center of each mound and ladle in the tomato sauce. Garnish with the shaved Parmesan cheese.

Serve immediately. This recipe is enough to get 6 people baked.

INGREDIENTS

6 cups water

1 ³/₄ cups of stone ground cornmeal

½ teaspoon of salt

¼ cup of Baked Butter

4 tablespoons of 'Oregano' Oil

3 cups of minced onion

3 large portobello mushrooms, chopped

4 cloves of garlic, minced

5 cups of marinara sauce

⅓ cup of sherry

1 teaspoon of crushed red pepper flakes

3 teaspoons of dried oregano

3 cups of green onions, chopped

½ cup of Parmesan cheese, grated

½ cup of Parmesan cheese, shaved

sea salt and pepper to taste

Secondo

The *secondo* is the heartiest and main course of an Italian meal, sometimes called the *piatto principale*.

Chicken Picatta 77

Italian Fish Stew 81

Rosemary Infused Steak 83

Filet with Balsamic Vinegar 85

Osso Bucco 87

Sausage Ragu 89

Sicilian Swordfish 91

Fennel with Prosciutto 93

Chicken Piccata

Originally made with veal, this dish is a treat for all the family

Season the chicken with salt and pepper. Put the flour in a bag and then add the chicken to the bag. Shake the chicken around while inside the bag so that it gets dredged with flour. Take the chicken out and shake off the excess flour. Set the chicken aside.

In a large, deep frying pan melt 2 tablespoons of the Baked Butter with 3 tablespoons of the 'Oregano' Oil over medium high heat. When the butter and oil start to sizzle, add 2 pieces of the chicken at a time and cook for 2 to 3 minutes until the chicken is browned. Turn the chicken over and cook the other side for another 2-3 minutes. Remove the chicken from the frying pan and transfer to plate.

Melt 2 more tablespoons of Baked Butter and add 2 tablespoons 'Oregano' Oil together. When the butter and oil start to sizzle, repeat the same process as above with the other 2 pieces of chicken. When they're browned on both sides, transfer them to the plate as well.

Add the lemon juice, the capers and the chicken stock to the same pan. Bring this sauce to a boil while scraping down brown bits from the sides and bottom of the pan. Add the fried chicken to the sauce in the frying pan. Bring the temperature up on the chicken by simmering the breasts for about 5 minutes.

INGREDIENTS

⅓ cup of Baked Butter
¼ cup of 'Oregano' Oil
½ cup of fresh lemon juice
½ cup of chicken stock
⅓ cup of capers
¼ cup of fresh parsley, chopped
2 skinless and boneless chicken
    breasts, cut in half and pounded
    (not too thin)
all-purpose flour, for dredging
sea salt and freshly ground black
    pepper

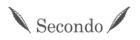

Secondo

Arrange the chicken on a platter. Add the rest of the remaining Baked Butter to the sauce in the frying pan and whisk briskly. Pour the sauce over the chicken and garnish with the chopped parsley.

Serve immediately. This recipe is enough to get 4 people baked.

Italian Fish Stew

A mix of subtle flavors
with a hearty punch

Cut the lobster and sole into 1-inch chunks. Combine the lobster and sole with the shrimp and lemon juice, then set aside.

Heat the 'Oregano' Oil in a large stew pot over medium heat. Add the garlic, celery and onions and cook them until translucent. Pour in the tomatoes, vinegar and wine and let the liquid come to a simmer. Cook for about 10 minutes.

Pour in the fish stock then add the marinated seafood and fish, basil, bay leaves and parsley. Simmer the stew for about 20 minutes, until the lobster has cooked through.

Season the stew with salt and pepper to taste.

Serve immediately with Crostini. This recipe is enough to get 4 people baked.

INGREDIENTS

⅓ cup of 'Oregano' Oil

4 cloves of garlic, minced

3 stalks of celery, chopped

1 large onion, sliced

15-ounce can of whole tomatoes

1 cup of balsamic vinegar

1 pound of lobster tails

1 pound of sole fillets

1 pound of medium shrimp, peeled
 and deveined

3 tablespoons of lemon juice

3 cups of Pinot Grigio

5 cups of fish stock

2 bay leaves

3 sprigs of fresh basil leaves, torn

4 tablespoons of fresh parsley,
 chopped

sea salt and pepper to taste

Rosemary Infused Steak
Straight from the
tables of Tuscany!

In a strong, Ziploc freezer bag, mix most of the 'Oregano' Oil , saving a little for later, with the vinegar, garlic and rosemary. Add the steak, seal the bag and refrigerate for about 12 hours, making sure to turn the bag several times.

Preheat the oven to 425°F, take the steak out of the fridge and bring it to room temperature. Heat a grill pan. Remove the steak from the marinade, pat dry with a clean dish towel and season with the salt and pepper. Rub all sides of the steak with the remaining 'Oregano' Oil.

Grill over moderately high heat until nicely charred on the top and bottom, which should take about 5 minutes each side. Transfer the steak to a glass baking sheet. Put the steak into the preheated oven and roast for about 25 minutes.

Test the steak by inserting an instant-read thermometer into it at the smaller section to make sure it registers 125°F.

Once cooked, transfer the steak to a cutting board and top the steak with the 2 tablespoons of Baked Butter. Let the steak rest for 10 minutes before slicing it across the grain. Serve immediately. This recipe is enough to get 4 to 6 people baked.

INGREDIENTS

½ cup of 'Oregano' Oil

2 tablespoons of Baked Butter

⅓ cup of rosemary, finely chopped

3-pound porterhouse steak, about 4
    inches thick

1 cup of balsamic vinegar

2 cloves of garlic, crushed

2 teaspoons of sea salt

2 teaspoons of black pepper,
    coarsely ground

olive oil

Filet with Balsamic Vinegar

A balsamic take on a classic dish

Cook slices of filet in the 'Oregano' Oil in a frying pan for about 3 minutes on each side. Set the tenderloin on a plate, then make the sauce in the same frying pan.

Mix the stock, balsamic vinegar, pepper, lemon juice and garlic together in the frying pan. Bring the liquid to a boil, and let it reduce a little.

Add the teaspoon of cornstarch and whisk it in. Once the sauce has thickened, whisk in the Baked Butter.

Put the tenderloin back into the frying pan along with any juices that may have escaped, cover and turn off the heat. Let the filets warm up, and then serve immediately garnished with the parsley.

This recipe is enough to get 4 people baked.

INGREDIENTS

4 slices of beef tenderloin, about an
   inch thick
¼ cup of 'Oregano' Oil
½ cup of beef stock
⅓ cup of balsamic vinegar
3 cloves garlic, finely minced
2 tablespoons of Baked Butter
1 teaspoon of cornstarch
⅓ cup of fresh parsley, chopped
a pinch of pepper
a squeeze of lemon juice

OSSO BUCCO

A Milanese specialty,
made with tender veal

Coat a large crock pot with the 'Oregano' Oil. Place the salt, pepper and tomato paste in the crock pot with the Chianti and beef stock and mix together well.

Season the veal shanks with salt and pepper and brown them in a frying pan, then add the meat and all the vegetables to the crock pot.

Cover the crock pot and cook on the low for 7-8 hours or on high temperature for 4-5 hours, or until the meat is tender.

Transfer the shanks and vegetables to a serving platter and cover the platter with foil in order to keep warm. Turn the crock pot to high and in a small bowl mix the flour with a few tablespoons of water until it's very smooth. Stir this liquid into cooking juices in the crock pot liquid to create a sauce.

Cover the crock pot and cook on high for about 15 minutes or until thickened. Serve the sauce over shanks and vegetables. Combine the parsley, lemon zest and lemon juice. Sprinkle this parsley combination over shanks.

Serve immediately, making sure the vegetables and shanks are still hot. Serve with Crostini. This recipe is enough to get 4 people baked.

INGREDIENTS

⅓ cup of 'Oregano' Oil

3 tablespoons of tomato paste

32-ounce can of crushed tomatoes

1 cup of beef stock

1 cup of Chianti

2 bay leaves

1 tablespoon of dried oregano

1 tablespoon of dried basil

1 tablespoon of dried parsley

5 garlic cloves, crushed

1 large onion, cut into thin wedges

4 large carrots, sliced

4 stalks of celery, chopped

4 large veal shanks

⅓ cup of flour

sea salt and black pepper to taste

zest of 1 large lemon

juice of ½ a large lemon

½ cup of fresh parsley, chopped

Sausage Ragu

Perfect for those rainy evenings
with a glass of red wine

Boil the sausage for 6 minutes in a large pot. Cook the sweet sausage first and then the spicy sausage. Allow each batch of sausage to cool.

Heat the 'Oregano' Oil in a large frying pan over medium heat. Stir in the onion, celery and garlic and cook until the onion is translucent; about 8 more minutes. Set the frying pan aside.

Pour the mixture into a crock pot. Add the sausage into the crock pot after crumbling it into bite-sized pieces. Put the frying pan back onto the stove over medium heat. Quickly pour the Chianti into the frying pan, and stir to dissolve the brown flavor bits stuck to the bottom of the pan.

When the pan bottom is clear, pour the Chianti into the slow cooker. Add the diced tomatoes, tomato sauce and salt to taste and mix it together well.

Set the heat on low, and cover the crock pot. Let the mixture cook for about 5 hours.

Pour the cream into the sausage mixture, stir, cover and cook for about 45 more minutes. Check the seasoning one more time before serving. Serve with Crostini. This recipe is enough to get 4 people baked.

INGREDIENTS

⅓ cup of 'Oregano' Oil

1 pound of sweet Italian sausage

1 pound of hot Italian sausage

2 large red onions, diced

6 stalks of celery, diced

5 cloves garlic, minced

½ cup of Chianti

16-ounce can of diced Roma
   tomatoes, not drained

16-ounce can of tomato sauce

1 cup of heavy cream

sea salt and pepper to taste

Sicilian Swordfish

A simple dish with lots of depth!

Preheat the broiler and, if necessary, move a rack to the top of your oven.

In a small bowl, mix the lemon juice with the sea salt until the salt dissolves. Stir in the oregano. Slowly whisk in the 'Oregano' Oil and season generously with pepper.

Broil the swordfish steaks under the broiler as close to the heat as possible. Broil for about 3 minutes until the steak is a nice color. Turn the steaks over and broil the other side for another 3 minutes or so until you get a nice color on that side as well.

Transfer the fish to a platter with a rim on it. Pierce each fish steak in several places with a fork to allow the sauce to penetrate.

Beat the sauce one last time before drizzling it over the fish. Serve at once.

Serve with crostini. This recipe is enough to get 4 people baked.

INGREDIENTS

⅓ cup of 'Oregano' Oil

4 swordfish steaks

¼ cup of fresh lemon juice

4 teaspoons of fresh oregano, chopped

sea salt and freshly ground pepper to taste

Fennel with Prosciutto

A delicate mix of flavors
that pack a punch

Heat the 'Oregano' Oil and the Baked Butter in a large frying pan. Add the chopped onion and let it cook over a low heat for about 10 minutes. Don't brown the onion.

Meanwhile, clean and cut the fennel bulbs into small cubes.

When the onions have cooked for 10 minutes, add the prosciutto to the frying pan and let it cook for 5 minutes. Then add the fennel and mix it all together. Sprinkle with salt and pepper and continue to cook for about 5 minutes. Add about 3 tablespoons of water to the frying pan in order to create a bit of a sauce. Cook the sauce and fennel for another 5 minutes.

Just before serving add the Asiago cheese and let it melt.

Serve immediately with Crostini. This recipe is enough to get 4 to 6 people baked.

INGREDIENTS

4 tablespoons of 'Oregano' Oil

2 tablespoons of Baked Butter

4 fennel bulbs

½ pound of prosciutto, sliced thinly

½ cup of Asiago cheese

1 onion, chopped finely

sea salt and black pepper to taste

Contorno

The *secondo* is most commonly served with the *contorno*, which are the side dishes. They usually consist of raw or cooked vegetables.

Potatoes with Tomato Sauce

A simple but heartwarming dish
that's the ultimate in comfort food

Peel the potatoes, cut them into slices and then put them into a large saucepan with half of the melted Baked Butter, and cook them gently until they are a good color.

Add the salt to the saucepan and then glaze the potatoes by adding the stock. Cook the potatoes until they are tender.

Arrange the potato slices on a dish, pour the heated marinara sauce over them, and add the rest of the melted Baked Butter and a squeeze of lemon juice. Season the dish to taste.

Serve immediately. This recipe is enough to get 4 to 6 people baked.

INGREDIENTS

6 large potatoes

½ cup of Baked Butter, melted

1 cup of marinara sauce, warmed

½ cup of stock

lemon

sea salt and black pepper to taste

Contorno

Carthusian Cabbage

So good, even the monks love it

In a large frying pan place the leeks, sardines and Baked Butter and cook on low heat until the leeks are soft. Add the cabbage to the frying pan, coat them in the butter, and cook gently so that the cabbage is hot and has absorbed all the flavor.

Transfer the cabbage to a serving dish or bowl, then add the grated Parmesan cheese and season to taste.

Serve immediately. This recipe is enough to get 4 to 6 people baked.

INGREDIENTS

1 small head of cabbage, boiled, cooled and sliced

½ cup of Baked Butter

3 leeks

1 or 2 sardines from a can

¼ cup of Parmesan cheese

sea salt and pepper to taste

Baked Italian

Italian Vegetable Salad

Get your five a day in a brand new way

In a large salad bowl, combine the broccoli, cauliflower, cherry tomatoes, cucumber, onion, carrots and both types of olives.

In a small bowl, whisk together the mayonnaise, vinegar, lemon juice, oil, Worcestershire sauce, oregano, basil, sugar and garlic until evenly combined.

Pour the salad dressing over the vegetable mixture and toss to coat. Cover and refrigerate for at least 4 hours. Stir in the mozzarella cheese just before serving.

This recipe is enough to get 6 people baked.

INGREDIENTS

1 head of broccoli, broken into florets

1 head of cauliflower, broken into florets

2 cups of cherry tomatoes

1 medium English cucumber, sliced

1 medium Vidalia onion, thinly sliced

1 cup of fresh carrots, sliced

1 cup of ripe olives, drained and sliced

½ cup of pimiento-stuffed olives

½ cup of mayonnaise

2 tablespoons of red wine vinegar

3 tablespoons of freshly squeezed lemon juice

⅓ cup of 'Oregano' Oil

1 teaspoon of Worcestershire sauce

1 teaspoon of dried oregano

1 teaspoon of dried basil

1½ teaspoons of white sugar

2 cloves of garlic, chopped

2 cups of mozzarella cheese, shredded

Sautéed Zucchini

A nutty veggie delight

Heat the 'Oregano' Oil in a large frying pan over a medium temperature. When the oil is hot, add the onions and sauté, stirring occasionally, for about 8 minutes, or until the onions have just turned golden brown.

Add the zucchini to the pan and sauté, stirring and turning frequently, for 8-10 minutes, until tender. Add the lemon juice and Pinot Grigio and reduce the heat to low. Stir in the almonds, salt and pepper and sauté, stirring constantly for 1 minute longer.

Remove pan from heat and transfer vegetables to a serving dish. This dish can be served hot or cold.

This recipe is enough to get 4 people baked.

INGREDIENTS

2 medium Vidalia onions, sliced

4 medium zucchini, sliced

½ cup of blanched almonds, toasted and slivered

⅓ cup of 'Oregano' Oil

2 teaspoons of freshly squeezed lemon juice

¼ cup of Pinot Grigio

sea salt and black pepper to taste

Layered Vegetable Casserole

Double dosed for extra pleasure!

Preheat oven to 375°F. Lightly grease a large loaf pan or casserole dish.

In a loaf pan, layer the vegetables in a decorative fashion, pouring a little Marijuana Milk, melted Baked Butter, salt and pepper and a little of the grated Parmesan and mozzarella in between each layer. Layer it like lasagna. I like to lay the sliced vegetables down, then put a layer of the raw spinach and then the Marijuana Milk and Parmesan and mozzarella cheeses, but feel free to do it any way you'd like.

Fill the loaf pan in this manner, and then bake it in the oven for 30 minutes.

Turn out and serve. Garnish with a dusting of Parmesan if you'd like. This recipe is enough to get 4 people baked.

INGREDIENTS

2 cups of sliced cauliflower, cooked until slightly tender then cooled

2 cups of sliced carrots, cooked until slightly tender then cooled

2 cups of sliced celery, cooked until slightly tender then cooled

1 bunch of spinach

3 tablespoons of Baked Butter, melted

½ cup of Marijuana Milk

½ cup of Parmesan

½ cup of mozzarella

sea salt and black pepper, to taste

Cauliflower Parmesan

A decadent dish that's rich and delicious

Preheat oven to 400°F. Grease a glass baking dish with a little of the Baked Butter.

Place cauliflower in prepared dish.

In a small bowl, stir together the Parmesan cheese, breadcrumbs, 2 tablespoons of the melted Baked Butter and parsley until mixed well. Sprinkle over cauliflower, tossing gently.

Bake for 15 minutes or until lightly browned and heated through. Remove from oven.

Transfer cauliflower to a serving dish and drizzle with remaining melted Baked Butter.

Serve immediately with Crostini. This recipe is enough to get 4 people baked.

INGREDIENTS

1 head of cauliflower, slightly cooked, cooled and broken into florets
½ cup of grated Parmesan cheese
½ cup of bread crumbs
½ cup of Baked Butter, melted
1 teaspoon of dried parsley

Dolce

After the *secondo* there is the *dolce*, or dessert.

Mandorla Cookies

Fall in love with these almondy bites!

Preheat oven to 400°F.

Cream the Baked Butter, sugar, egg and almond extract together in a large mixing bowl. Add the flour, baking powder and milk then blend together well.

Roll small amounts of dough for each cookie. Roll each ball between your palms like you would for peanut butter cookies or even meatballs.

Roll the balls in the chopped almonds and place them on greased cookie sheets. Make indentation with your thumb or the back of a spoon and fill the dent with jam.

Bake for 12 to 15 minutes. Two cookies should get you baked.

½ cup of Baked Butter

1 cup of sugar

1 egg

1 teaspoon of almond extract

2 cups of all-purpose flour, sifted

1 teaspoon of baking powder

2 tablespoons of Marijuana Milk

1 cup of chopped almonds

⅓ cup of apricot jam

Génoise Cake

Enjoy the taste of Genoa in every single bite!

Preheat oven to 350°F.

Grease two 8-inch round cake pans with Baked Butter, then line each pan with parchment paper and grease it as well. Lightly flour the pans and the paper.

Sift together the flour, 2 tablespoons of the sugar and all of the salt onto a piece of wax paper. Do this two more times.

Break the eggs into a large mixing bowl and set the bowl over a pan of hot (but not boiling) water. Add the sugar to the eggs and whisk until the mixture feels warm (but not hot) to the touch. It should be around your body temperature.

Once the mixture is warm, use a hand mixer on medium speed to beat the mixture until it becomes pale yellow in color and falls off the end of the whisk attachment in long ribbons. Add the vanilla extract and mix. Add about ¼ of the flour mixture to the beaten eggs and fold it in. Continue to add the flour in quarters, folding it in each time.

Place about 1 cup of the batter into a bowl along with the melted Baked Butter and mix together. Add this combination back into the main batter

INGREDIENTS

6 tablespoons of Baked Butter, melted (plus more for pan)

1½ cup of all-purpose flour (pan)

1 cup of sugar

6 large eggs

¼ teaspoon of salt

1 teaspoon of pure vanilla extract

FOR BUTTERCREAM ICING

½ cup of shortening, softened

½ cup of Baked Butter, softened

5 cups of sifted icing sugar

¼ cup of Marijuana Milk

½ teaspoon of vanilla extract

and fold it in.

Divide the batter between the prepared pans.

Immediately bake for about 25 minutes or until the tops are a light brown.
Cool the cakes in the pans on a rack for about 10 minutes and then invert the pans onto a rack. It's best to invert it again onto another rack so that it cools with the top up.

Let the cakes cool completely before cutting or icing them with the Buttercream Icing.

FOR BUTTERCREAM ICING:

In a large bowl, cream together the Baked Butter, shortening and vanilla. Blend in the sugar, 1 cup at a time, beating well after each addition.

Beat in the Marijuana Milk, and continue mixing until light and fluffy. Keep icing covered until ready to decorate.

One slice of cake, topped with this icing, is enough to get you baked.

Tiramisu

The unbeatable combination of coffee, cheese and chocolate

In a medium bowl, beat the egg yolks with sugar and vanilla until smooth and light yellow. Fold mascarpone into yolk mixture. Set aside.

In a small bowl dissolve the instant coffee with the Cannabis Campari.

Dip ladyfingers briefly in the coffee mixture and arrange 12 of them in the bottom of an 8 x 8-inch dish. Spread half the mascarpone mixture over the ladyfingers. Repeat with remaining ladyfingers and mascarpone.

Garnish with cocoa and chocolate curls. Refrigerate several hours or overnight.

To make the chocolate curls, use a vegetable peeler and run it down the edge of the chocolate bar.

This recipe is enough to get 4 to 6 people baked.

INGREDIENTS

3 egg yolks

¼ cup of white sugar

2 teaspoons of vanilla extract

1¼ cups of mascarpone cheese

24 ladyfingers

1 cup of Cannabis Campari

1 tablespoon of instant espresso (or instant coffee)

1 teaspoon of unsweetened cocoa powder, for dusting

1-ounce square or bar of semisweet chocolate

Coffee Gelato

The fantastic Italian version of ice cream
that melts in your mouth

Whisk the egg yolks and sugar together in large bowl to combine.

Bring the Marijuana Milk to a boil in heavy saucepan.

Very slowly whisk the hot Marijuana Milk into the egg mixture to combine. You have to do this very slowly so that the egg yolk doesn't cook. Whisk in the espresso mixture.

Return the egg and coffee mixture to the saucepan.

Stir over medium low heat until the egg mixture turns into a custard and thickens. The custard should leave a path on the back of the spoon when you draw your finger across. This takes about 6 to 8 minutes. Do not let it boil.

Refrigerate the custard until cold, which should take more than 3 hours. Freeze in a covered container. If you have an ice cream maker then process the gelato in the ice cream maker according to manufacturer's instructions.

This recipe is enough to get 6 to 8 people baked.

INGREDIENTS

10 large egg yolks

2 cups of sugar

3 cups of Marijuana Milk

1 tablespoon of instant espresso powder, dissolved in ½ cup hot water

Lemon Panna Cotta

A light, creamy traditional Italian dessert

Sprinkle the entire package of gelatin over 2 tablespoons of heavy cream in a small bowl. Let it soften for about 5 minutes.

Combine the Marijuana Milk, sugar and vanilla in a saucepan over a low heat. Bring this mixture to a simmer for a couple of minutes then remove the saucepan from the heat.

Stir the gelatin and cream mixture in a saucepan until it's all dissolved.

Place the yogurt in medium bowl and whisk until smooth. Gradually whisk the Marijuana Milk mixture and lemon juice into the yogurt.

Pour mixture into six small ramekins. Chill for about 4 hours or until set.

For the topping, toss the fruit, Vector Vodka, Cannabis Campari and sugar together with the lemon zest. Refrigerate for at least 20 minutes.

To remove the Panna Cotta from the ramekins, run a sharp knife around the edges then invert the ramekin onto a plate.

Top with fruit mixture and serve.

This recipe is enough to get 6 people baked.

INGREDIENTS

1 envelope of unflavored gelatin

2 cups of Marijuana Milk

2 tablespoons of heavy cream

½ cup of sugar

2 teaspoons of pure vanilla extract

2¼ cups of plain yogurt (preferably Greek style)

2 teaspoons of freshly squeezed lemon juice

For the Fruit Topping:

1 cup of raspberries, red and golden

2 cups of mixed strawberries or blueberries

2 peaches, peeled, thinly sliced

2 teaspoons of sugar

1 ounce of Vector Vodka

1 ounce of Cannabis Campari

1 tablespoon of lemon zest

Oregano, Lavender and Vanilla Bean Ice Cream

A delicious combination of savory and sweet

To prepare the oregano puree, fill a small bowl with ice water. Set aside. Bring a small saucepan of water to a boil.

Blanch the oregano and lavender for 10 seconds in the boiling water. Remove the herbs with a slotted spoon and quickly plunge into the ice water. Strain the herbs, then puree in a blender with ½ cup of water, 1 cup of sugar and honey. Set the puree aside.

To prepare the ice cream, combine the Marijuana Milk, cream and ¾ cup of sugar in a heavy saucepan and bring the mixture to a simmer.

Whisk together the egg yolks and the remaining ¼ cup of sugar.

Remove the Marijuana Milk mixture from the heat and add a little to the egg yolk mixture to warm it up, whisking constantly to keep the yolks from cooking.

Once warm, slowly pour the egg yolk mixture back into the hot Marijuana Milk, whisking it constantly as you pour.

Return the mixture to the stove and cook over low heat until the egg turns into a custard and thickens. The custard should leave a path on the

INGREDIENTS

1 cup of oregano, packed

¼ cup of lavender

½ cup of water

1 cup of sugar (for puree)

2 teaspoons of honey

3 cups of Marijuana Milk

1 cup of heavy cream

1 cup of sugar, divided (for ice cream)

10 large egg yolks

1 teaspoon of pure vanilla extract

back of the spoon when you draw your finger across. This takes about 6 to 8 minutes. Do not let it boil.
Stir in the herb puree.

Refrigerate the custard until cold, which should take more than 3 hours.

Freeze in a covered container. If you have an ice cream maker then process the ice cream in the ice cream maker according to manufacturer's instructions.

This recipe is enough to get 6 to 8 people baked.

Caffè and Digestivo

Caffè (or coffee, to you and me) is often drunk at the end of an Italian meal, even after the digestive. Unlike in North America, Italian meals do not have milky coffees or drinks after meals.

The *digestivo*, if served after the coffee, is the drink to conclude the meal. The drinks served at this time are meant to ease digestion after a long meal.

Laced Limoncello

Not the lemonade your nonna used to make!

Shave off the yellow part of the lemon rinds using a potato peeler. Put these lemon rinds in a large glass bottle or jar and add the Vector Vodka.

Cover the bottle or jar with plastic wrap as well as the lid to prevent any alcohol from evaporating. Let the bottle sit for 2 weeks at room temperature.

Boil the water in a large saucepan. Remove the pan from the heat and add sugar. Stir until all the sugar has dissolved and let the mixture cool.

Strain the lemon rinds from the 2-week-old Vector Vodka mix. Add the vodka to the sugared water.

Fill the bottle or jar back up with the new mixture and cover with plastic wrap as well as the lid. Set the bottle aside for an additional 10 days, again at room temperature.

After 10 days, the Laced Limoncello is ready. It is best served chilled.

For every alcoholic beverage you drink make sure you drink a pint of water – and this goes for alcohol without weed in it, too! One glass should be enough to get one person baked.

INGREDIENTS

8 cups of Vector Vodka

20 lemons (Sorrento lemons, if possible)

4 cups of sugar

4 cups of water

Angelo Azzurro

A blue dream over ice

Pour the ingredients into a cocktail shaker and shake well. Serve in an ice filled rock glass or a martini glass. No garnish needed.

For every alcoholic beverage you drink make sure you drink a pint of water – and this goes for alcohol without weed in it, too! One glass should be enough to get one person baked.

INGREDIENTS

2 ounces of Ganja Gin
1 ounce of Triple Sec or Cointreau
½ ounce of Blue Curacao

Laced Lemon Martini

Everyone's favorite drink laced with a little lemon

Pour the ingredients into a cocktail shaker filled with ice and shake well. Serve in a martini glass with a lemon twist as garnish.

For every alcoholic beverage you drink make sure you drink a pint of water – and this goes for alcohol without weed in it, too! One glass should be enough to get one person baked.

INGREDIENTS

½ ounce Laced Limoncello

1 ounce Vector Vodka

1 lemon twist

Hazelnut Martini

You'll go nuts for this version
of a classic cocktail!

Rim a martini glass with brown sugar.

Pour the ingredients into a cocktail shaker filled with ice and shake well. Strain into a martini glass and garnish with an orange slice.

For every alcoholic beverage you drink make sure you drink a pint of water – and this goes for alcohol without weed in it, too! One glass should be enough to get one person baked.

INGREDIENTS

1 ¼ ounces of Vector Vodka

¾ ounce of Frangelico

¾ ounce of Cointreau

1 ounce of half-and-half

Tiramisu Martini

The perfect combination
of coffee and dessert

Rim a martini glass with hot chocolate mix.

Pour the ingredients into a cocktail shaker filled with ice and shake well.

Strain into a martini glass and garnish with a chocolate curl, or as shown in the photo.

For every alcoholic beverage you drink make sure you drink a pint of water – and this goes for alcohol without weed in it, too! One glass should be enough to get one person baked.

INGREDIENTS

1¼ ounces of Vector Vodka

¾ ounce of coffee liqueur

¾ ounce of Amaretto

1 ounce of half-and-half

Café Polonaise

A drink with a tang!

Put the two sugar cubes in a coffee cup or espresso cup.

Add the Vector Vodka, coffee and lemon juice to the cup and stir.

If you're using the cream, float it; do not stir or mix it.

For every alcoholic beverage you drink make sure you drink a pint of water – and this goes for alcohol without weed in it, too! One glass should be enough to get one person baked.

Café Pucci

A treat served warm, and sure to melt the coldest of hearts

Put the brown sugar in an espresso cup.

Add the Vector Vodka, almond liqueur and the coffee and stir.

If you are using the cream, float it; do not stir or mix it.

For every alcoholic beverage you drink make sure you drink a pint of water – and this goes for alcohol without weed in it, too! One glass should be enough to get one person baked.

INGREDIENTS

1 ounce of Vector Vodka

½ ounce of almond liqueur

1 teaspoon of brown sugar

1 demitasse of espresso

cream (optional)

Café Bella

Just the thing for an afternoon pick-me-up!

Place the Vector Vodka, Frangelico, Irish cream liqueur and coffee into an espresso cup and stir.

If you're using the cream, float it; do not stir or mix it.

For every alcoholic beverage you drink make sure you drink a pint of water – and this goes for alcohol without weed in it, too! One glass should be enough to get one person baked.

INGREDIENTS

1 ounce of Vector Vodka
½ ounce of Frangelico
½ ounce of Irish cream liqueur
1 demitasse of espresso
cream (optional)

Index

Baked Italian

Index